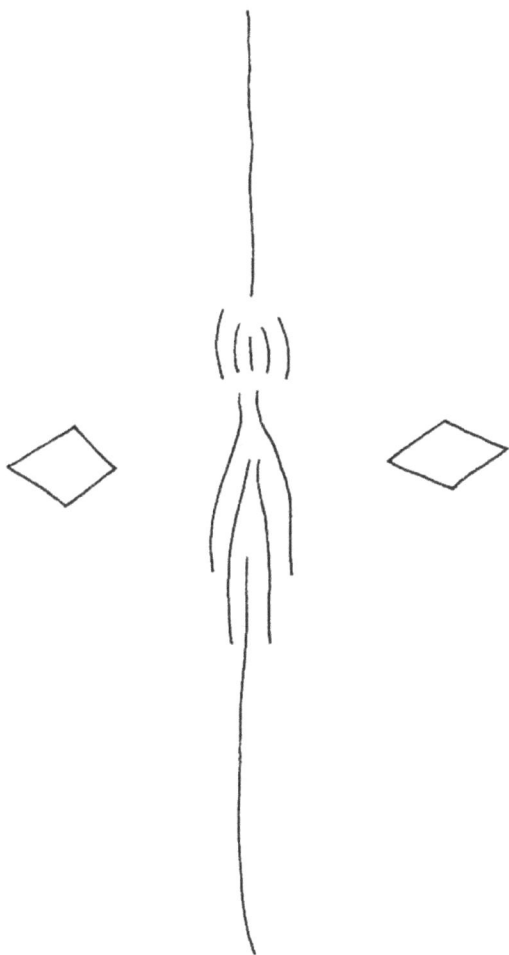

Pearly Gates Press
Volume 1

Pearly Gates Press
Volume 1

Solar System Secrets
12 Angelic Scrolls of the Atman
Heavenly Data Transmissions
Archangel Christopher

by Christopher Moors

ISBN-10: 0985697903
ISBN-13: 978-0-9856979-0-7

Published 2005 by the Creative Cosmos

Printed in the United States of America

Dedicated to the women in my family,

My sisters, Stacy and Kim
My mother, Geraldine &
My grandmothers, Donna and Virginia

Table of Contents

Solar System Secrets

12 Angelic Scrolls of the Atman

Heavenly Data Transmissions

Archangel Christopher

Solar System Secrets

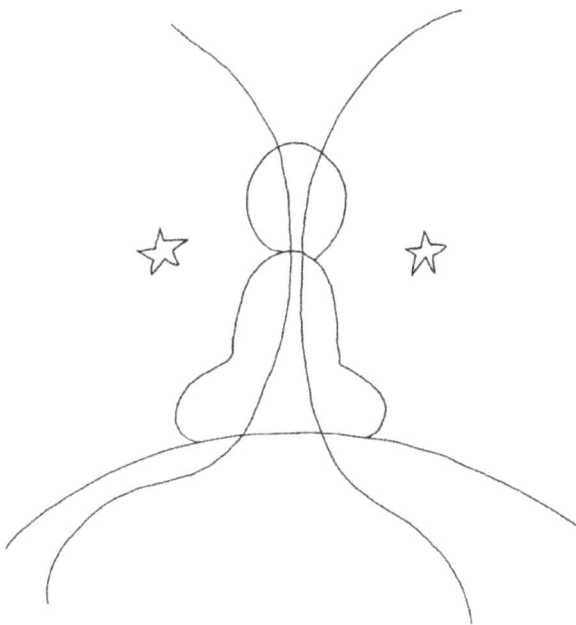

Solar System Secrets as Told by the Sun

The pyramid builders first interacted with humanity's 3rd generation on the planet Mars. It was generally known and accepted that 'aliens' were coming and going frequently. Since it was a part of everyday life, not many found it odd.

The artificial moons Demos and Phobos were 'Eyes in the Sky' put in place by the rulers to enforce societal law. Culture was much like the Ancient Egypt that you have caricature descriptions of in your text books. In fact, the seeds of this nuance come from Pleiades where the Astral Version of this Theosophy resides.

It was not war that destroyed the civilization of Mars. Their orbit simply moved too far out to sustain the balance that they had enjoyed for 18,000 years. The water began to dry up and food could no longer grow. Air was becoming toxic as the shaking of the magnetic field caused volcanoes to blow. The remaining survivors came up with the 'Adam and Eve project' to save their species and then turned to the pyramid builders for help.

Placing representative DNA samples in

transportable containers, the pyramid builders offered to deliver the specimens to the next red planet in, Earth. Ever since then, they have been interfering with the development of humanity. On Mars, the people knew the pyramid builders and were considered partners on an equal basis. On Earth, the pyramid builders have used the people's forgetfulness to enslave them and make them into servants. Opportunists above all else, it was their cruelty and disregard for spirit which enabled the Giza monuments to be built.

In a previous incarnation, Hitler was a pharaoh and representative of the pyramid builders. He remembered these times and their dramatic magnitude. He could not escape the megalomaniacal visions that consumed him. With like disregard for the suffering of incarnated spirit, he drove the people by the whip of his stinging words and deathly serious sense of purpose.

Now as the Earth begins to move out past the line of equilibrium that Mars did in that age so long ago, humanity has to consider something new. Put together all the experience that you have gained and create the Utopian civilization on Venus. It is not coincidental that humanity named her after the Goddess of Love. She will be the realization of all of our dreams – the true lady liberty. Once the final transition has occurred, blessings will be upon you and peace will at last remain for a long enough period to enjoy it.

Eventually you will use the moons of Saturn as a platform to the rest of the Universe. Allow yourselves to think much bigger. Your technology will follow your vision and conviction. There are many ways to look at things and much better propulsion systems on the horizon. Whatever you do, do not take the pyramid builders with you to Venus.

Solar System Secrets II

About 65,000,000 BC, a Celestial Noah's Ark arrived at Earth from deep within the Orion Constellation, to save the DNA of the remaining Thunder Lizards from the upcoming extinction event. The Orion Mission intended to relocate Dinosaur DNA to an Earth-like planet in the Draco System. The initial harvesting was a success and the subsequent planting of the foreign species on the planet Jalon carried forth without incident.

Unfamiliar with the strong environmental accommodation of lizards, the Orion Sentient Beings were caught off-guard while during their continuing observations they noticed a change in the behavior of the flourishing creatures. Over many years the thinner atmosphere of Jalon caused the Reptilian bodies to shrink and their vibratory frequency to rise into what we would call the lower astral planes or the first layer of the 4th dimension.

Without dense gravity pushing blood flow down, their brain synapses became more supple, extending into a cerebellum and just the first inklings of a cerebrum capable of self-conscious thought. The transition enabled them to evolve a sense of tool-making in a few thousand years into something well beyond humanity's most current technology. The instinctual homing device in their medulla called them back out to the stars. Having the extra advantage of being just into the 4th Dimension, they developed the means to travel light years of space in a fraction of the time it would take for even the highest potential 3 D craft.

Soon they felt their way back to the Solar System of their origin, but were surprised to find out that they could no longer access this area of the Universe because their bodies no longer coincided with the frequency. After much quarrelling amongst themselves, they decided to inhabit unconscious human bodies and try to maintain 3D form by eating meat, drinking blood, and absorbing the energy of weak 3D beings.

Still feeling like the planet Earth was theirs, they got involved in the political affairs of men, taking over dominant positions and herding terrestrials to do their bidding. Thus began 1000s of years of slave rule by divine kingship without recorded history. Great pyramidal monuments were built in Egypt to honor their Orion Saviors. Lurking in the shadows and maintaining allegiances within

Solar System Secrets

secret societies, they have been able to work
largely unopposed to this day.

Solar System Secrets III

All planets have consciousness. People must speak in the language of any given planet to successfully communicate and not have the preposterous expectation that planets come right out and use human words with a human mouth in order to confirm meaning transaction. Tune into the frequency and then exchange Understanding through Intention. The Music of the Spheres is a reality that can be experienced, not just a metaphor for something more mundane. You can hear the sound of each planetary being emerge gracefully from the Aum.

Planets reveal the nature of their ideas in the moons that encircle them. Companionship desire either draws a body close or splits a body off. Earth chooses only one celestial partner in order to reflect the Intimacy for which Her Soul School is renown throughout the astral realms. Friendship and loyalty are character development offshoots of this root principle that many Spirits claim they developed while incarnated there.

These magnificent orbiting entities are not simply 3D objects in a 3D world. Several of them rise as high as the 5th or 6th dimensions. We find life in the higher dimensions on gaseous Jupiter. There are a multitude of Angels in Jupiter's clouds and they are well aware of life on Earth.

Saturn expresses abundance with a moon family that sings a noble chorus of elation amplified millions of times by the tiny ones who make up the rings. Like a school of inanimate fish, these mini manifestations, demonstrate that size and history are not as important as form and destiny. Young in development and still very close to the Source, Wisdom and Joy are their beatific display and the unique quality of this area of the Universe.

Each planet has a magnetic field as does each person. Humans are always influenced by the field of the Earth, but also exchange vibes everyday with many planets. Not only do the planets influence people, but people influence planets. In fact, planets have even created a kind of "reverse astrology" to consider the human effect upon them!

It is foolish for humanity to look for signs of "life" based on itself as a definition. When you have been given the unique ability to act as a crossroads to all realms, why would you seek to limit what you allow yourselves to perceive?

Solar System Secrets

Intrinsically, humans have the ability to tune down dimensions – communicating with the animals in animal speak, or up dimensions – communicating with heavenly bodies in abstract musical visions.

Your Solar Center can transport messages to other Stars who can then deliver them to planets in their systems and the entities within that Space whichever dimension they reside in. Sometimes when people on Earth have eaten aptly called Magic Mushrooms, they have been more readily able to contact these beings in other dimensions because their third eye and heart centers open, and there is much less resistance to the process. These were left for you by cosmic travelers from Pleiades who wanted you to remember where you truly come from.

2

Solar System Secrets IV

7 Sisters become 7 Chakras making up 7 colors of the rainbow. They branch into nerve systems sheathed within a protective layer of skin. Earth and Water meet in such perfect balance that Air and Fire can not help but breathe them into life.

The Pleiadian connection to Ancient Atlantis and the Golden Era of Egyptian Civilization must be emphasized. Atlantis strikes such a wondrous chord in the heart of humans because it hearkens back to a time when souls remembered where they came from. Starlight still twinkling in their mind, they made use of crystals to deepen their meditation and energize resource transference devices.

From the Pyramidal-shaped Crystal Temple in the Center of the City, Atlantians freely traveled from this planet through a Grand Star Gate left for them by their Seed Planters from the Pleiadian Star System. Where they went was not a physical place. The Angelic Pleiadians exist on the 6th dimension, so in order to communicate with the 3rd dimension, the symbolic language of the 4th dimension dream plane is used as a crossroads. This process is familiar to any who has

Channeled Spirits, has had Lucid Dreams, OBE's, or to those who have undertaken a Vision Quest as described by Shamans.

Surrounding the Crystal Temple in nature modeled architectural geometry, were 12 Celestial Temples representing the Archetypes of Ancient Astrology. Within each ornately adorned structure was held one of 12 Lesser Star Gates. When the Catastrophic Events began to occur as both scientist and mystic alike predicted, many Atlantians permanently left the 3rd dimension through the magic portals. The 12 Caretakers of the Celestial Temples were left behind to destroy their corresponding Star Gates, as Princess Atalanta herself remained to ensure elimination of the Grand Star Gate.

The long planned procedure was to annihilate all 13 Gates so that no Terrestrials of Gaia would ever get their hands on this awesome Cosmic Technology. Following completion of demolition, they were to fall upon their newly polished, 100 hours of sunlight charged, silver swords and give up the ghost. All did as was predestined but One.

The most Intelligent of the Caretakers, who had secretly established a cult of his own, ordered 6 loyal men to take the Star Gate under his

protection to a waiting ship. He and his followers
had spent the last 7 years building this stalwart
vessel after the Caretaker had a divine revelation
about founding a Great Empire following the
demise of Atlantis. With 20 men and 30 women,
they boldly set sail as the remnants of the island
fell into the Sea.

Many years later near what would some day be
called Alexandria, a 21 year old Egyptian scribe
name Nefu found several broken pieces of what
appeared to be a relic from some forgotten land,
wash up on the morning sand. He hurriedly
carried them back home to his older brother who
was blacksmith to the Pharaoh. With much effort,
they forged the pieces together to form a very
large incomplete circle. Satisfied that they had
done all they could, they brought the strange and
wonderful artifact before the Ruler of the Ancient
World.

Mighty Pharaoh decided on transporting the
intriguing item to the Great Temple to consult
with High Priest Termus. Before they even
arrived, a running Termus met them shouting, "I
have heard. I have heard. We must find the
missing piece!" A major effort was immediately
undertaken to scour the beach. By the time the
piece was recovered, the main body of the

mysterious circular structure had been propped up in the front of the Temple under the watchful Eye of Ra.

When the Final Stone was put into place, the Star Gate reawakened with a lurch, causing a collective gasp as it became electrically invigorated and began emitting a soft steady hum. Soon the first brave warriors made contact with the Pleiadians, interpreted their Symbols according to themselves, and interwove these messages with accurate depictions of a Self-Conscious Sun to create a Mystical Awareness Method that lasted 4000 years.

Solar System Secrets V - Planet Minerva

Long before life was in its present stage on Planet Earth, there was a bustling crossroads in the Center Orbit of the Solar System. Situated between Mars and Jupiter, Planet Minerva was a well known stopping point for Galaxy Travelers. Among the finest Artistic Ideas in Creation, she was the crowning jewel of an already elegant and evolving Planetary Family.

Looking much like an older sister to Mars, Earth, and Venus, Minerva was strong and noble. Her resonant music reached to such transcendent heights that Saturn once had to beg her to pause for fear of losing himself in its beauty. Before now it has been too painful to reveal something which is suppressed in all of the planets. How we lost our Loved One and the resulting Trauma we have all felt will now be brought forward so Healing can be found and we can return Minerva into our Hearts.

The outer reason She was lost, was a horrific crime by a marauding group of twisted aliens based in a little known region of space just over the shoulder of Perseus. They did not invent the technology that allowed them the luxury of speed

Pearly Gates Press Volume 1

with which to visit Minerva's Sacred Sphere. In
one of our Free Universe's twists of Time's
Unfolding, these bearers of malcontent were
bumbling their way over a rocky mountain pass
on their home planet Tak when a newly opened
fissure deep within the parched landscape
revealed a perfectly preserved Star Craft.

The ship belonged to a Race of Beings called the
Prontonians. They were joyful beings who were
frequent visitors to Minerva. They also had a
habit of leaving spare shuttles underground on
any planet they ever explored. When the filthy
residents of Tak scampered into the ship and
started pressing buttons, it happened to engage
the autopilot to Minerva. Prior to this, Minerva
had been protected as an Enchanted place. Word
of Her Energies which Foster Self-Realization
traveled quietly throughout the Universe as a
Transmission of Truth to those who Understood
such things.

When the Takians landed on Minerva, Destiny
took a Cold form. They exited the craft and
breathing the rejuvenating air, became stronger in
their chaotic projections. Soon they were
following the pristine paths that had been tended
to for Countless Millennia by Cosmic Monks from
20 Star Systems to the Echoing Thought Palace.

With disregard for all decorum, they burst in and together forcefully began chanting, "NO NO NO NO NO NO NO" in their Mind. Minerva having been Vulnerable and caught by surprise shrieked as if the Crooked Knife of the Undead had just pierced Her Soul. "NO NO NO NO NO", they found the worst possible thought and just kept amplifying it.

The outer situation became so serious so fast because the inner harmony had been allowed to degenerate. Fascinated with Saturn's Newly Forming Rings, and marveling at the Many Moons of Jupiter, the System had begun to take for Granted the Qualities which Minerva had embodied for so long. Mars bustled with Life and Earth was beginning to stir, while Uranus, and Neptune whistled into higher and higher planes of reality. No matter what She did, Minerva couldn't get Our attention anymore.

By the time the System realized what was happening with the Takians, it was too late. Unable to bear a life of Endless "NO's", Minerva used her remaining strength to pull the Comet Re Sa straight into the Center of her Planetary body. Exploding with a force here-to-fore unknown to the rest of the System, we all recoiled and have held our collective breaths ever since, allowing things to settle down. It has been long enough that we must face the Collective Denial that brought about Minerva's Demise.

Her Spirit was blasted into as many pieces as Her body. Now her Heavenly Family must Unite their Wills and bring what she represented back into Existence so that a New Body might form. Say "YES YES YES" and She will return.

Solar System Secrets VI

Our Solar System was originally conceived of as having 9 planets: Mercury, Venus, Earth, Mars, Minerva, Jupiter, Saturn, Uranus, and Neptune. Each was allowed to have as many moons as imagination could facilitate. Mercury, moonlike himself, chose to bask in the full glory of the Solar Wind. Venus decided to wait to have children until after humanity arrives. She will then attract 3 new companions to share life with all involved. Earth's single Moon awakens Love and Intimacy, giving birth to the feminine in men and wisdom in women. Mars' 2 observatory satellites left over from the human era still hold their close line to the deserted planet.

Minerva spent all of her energy balancing the inner planets and outer planets while playing host to many celestial events so didn't have time for little ones. The Galactic Council met there once long ago and have thus far held back revelation of these events. They do so only because they are waiting for the predestined sign which gives acquiescence to the full revelation of all past in the present.

The Galilean moons of Jupiter: Io, Europa,

Ganymede, and Callisto, were a higher level of
actualization, bringing forth almost planet like
worlds to wander around a mini sun. Speckling
the background are companion creations
captured by all of them to enlarge their fantastic
family. One day they will be released into space
to grow their own version of reality. They have
earned this by fulfilling their destiny with honor
and nobility.

Saturn has more than a dozen icy friends, with
the largest Titan much like a cosmic Babe the Blue
Ox (legendary partner of lumberjack Paul
Bunyan). Oft underrated Uranus longs to be a
guide and gentle nurturing spirit to Americans in
particular. Uranus embodies something they
desperately need, the ability to let down their
guard and the relaxedness to have humor about
ones lot in life. Many moons have quietly sought
vigil around this tilted giant, and have felt lucky
to have this gorgeous beauty largely to
themselves.

Giving equal thought-force to each world in this
Creation, Neptune was to round things out with a
depth of fervor devoted in service to harmonic
resonance. Triton, joined with Pluto, who for
some time was content to revolve around his
brother, in looking after the younger and smaller

Solar System Secrets

worlds at the end of the system. The noble auras were shattered when Pluto began His UNHOLY INTRIGUE.

As Minerva's Grace disappeared after the Great Disaster and we all receded in mourning, He used the magnetic absence to begin rallying the small worlds around his dark teaching. Pluto enacted His modest Will and began to pull them away from Neptune with intent of becoming the new 9th planet. Neptune felt a tearing of his Mind and pulled back in fury to reclaim his rightful satellites born from centuries of his own ponderous dreams. Still marked by a dark spot on his surface, Neptune fell into a profound sadness at his loss. Ashamed and isolated but for his own devoted apprentice Charon, Pluto would never return to the soothing comfort of his brother's Love, but maintains to this day, the dubious honor of being the cold and lonely last planet with a puzzling oblong orbit.

Solar System Secrets VII

The Center Star with which you are familiar, heretofore referred to by His ancient name – RA, is not without companionship in the Milky Way Galaxy. The Creative force which springs forth all things and has a peculiar propensity towards duality found it necessary to give birth to a twin of the Sun we know and love. Though gender is not specific with celestial bodies, even they tend to lean towards one or the other sexual identity. Ra as we have gathered throughout the centuries is Male, and Ro the twin is Female.

This plays out in the planetary Creations each manifests to fill out their own families. Ra has surrounded Himself with planets that balance Him by cumulatively being a bit more on the female side. Jupiter being the main male figure in Ra's system mainly looks after the outer planets. The female Earth is the focus of Ra's Love even as Minerva was before and Venus someday shall be.

Ro surrounds Herself with planets a bit more male. Currently "Hope" and "Justice" are her planetary Love focus, as her other 6 planets (Ro's System has 8 total, with a wide variety of moons) play mostly amongst themselves. Being a nonidentical twin, Her system although similar has many different qualities than Ra's. The music of Her spheres often expresses melody and emotion, while Ra's emphasizes harmony and wisdom.

Two bright eyes always looking outward towards their systems, they are One at a higher level of Consciousness in the same manner as the Third Eye unifies the Human Eyes. Through this inward flow, the Source of all of Life monitors their progress even as it sustains the rest of the Universe. A series of Creators and Creations, the chain comes down to the writer of this message who is a Creation of the Earth who is a Creation of the Sun who is a Creation of the Source. The Great Invigorator Aum flows through us all.

Many times the Twin Sun partnership has manifested its implications on Minerva, Earth and in Ro's living planets. Famous twins such as Romulus and Remus have founded whole empires reflecting the strength of starlight which makes embodied Life possible. Occasionally, singular figures will rise up and take on characteristics of one or the other Sun, but missing their other half, will be overbalanced and often burn out in a blaze of glory.

Following their own many millennium orbits, Ra

and Ro are coming closer every day. For years their paths led further away from each other, but the corner has been turned and their light is beginning to intermingle at the fringes. This is precisely why the people on Earth who are able to receive the bounty of this interaction are starting to wake up to their Soul's Greater Journey. As usual the power structure will try to crack down harder and harder, but will one day suddenly be revealed as the impotent Homo Sapiens that they are while Homo Superius (Universal Humanity) will be given their rightful place as Gods on Earth until they leave their shells and return home to the Stars.

12 Angelic Scrolls
of the Atman

An Angelic Scroll of the Atman

Pyramid power flows through one who undergoes silent treatment. Balancing anticipation with cool patience, each step forward is a miracle. Trust in source-love.

A single eye springs forth a myriad of possibilities each with its own unique attitude. Though many, we are one. Though one, we are many. Indivisible, we seek to hide.

The spectacular over-soul blasts the vacant vessel with a million marvelous frequencies. Light becomes nerves, then skin and hair. Blink, breath, and walk around as a myth.

The newness of now pierces yesterday's blues. Change is the state of one who gets what its like to be alive. Whistle me a tune or keep to yourself. A true gift keeps on giving.

Torments in the mind keep some from expressing what they know deep down inside. Sell out your dream and when you cross over, the multitudes will show you the error.

When the most important thing in your life has a

33

strange geometry, all is lost for nothing.
Resonating bad vibes you spray a psychic stink
that drives even your best friends away.

The rain knows the melancholy ache of bearing
the lonely cross of truth. Rainbows are created to
give us hope. Each moment of pain ripens us for
the path. Home is 'here'.

Even the most cynical of us would smile
spontaneously upon realizing that the biggest
joke of all was the one being played on you by
you. In the end there is no harm.

A Second Angelic Scroll of the Atman

Spark of intelligence. First transmission. No entity to respond. Situation untenable. Flame became two. Love and fear. Water came with wind.

Pulsing blossom. Respond accordingly. Extinguish wrong turns. Cruise circuits, then release. Every time the crow flies, a straight line is born. Mind the omen.

Soul gems shine when illuminated. Gather moss, then treat the wound. Cry raindrops and refresh the morning. Pray for the irrevocable. Question all things off limits.

Attention is as important as intention. Scrutinize the finest details while exalting in the luxury of being unencumbered. Space is a shadow of time.

Friendliness is not to be misconstrued as naivety. Nobody fits the description. Leave alone what you don't want to deal with. Inevitability can be slowed.

Validation is not necessary. Loneliness will always be temporary. Suffering lasts as long as it needs to. No gesture goes unnoticed. Eyes are everywhere.

Silence is the backdrop to all noise. Under even the heaviest rock you may discover salamanders. Seek to find. Failure is giving up. Kings and queens stand tall.

A Third Angelic Scroll of the Atman

Discovery is facilitated when OPEN enters your subconscious. Unravel the mummy of mommy and dad. Disaster awaits those living up to expectations.

Moonglow romances melt the young. Sturdiness is needed for the journey of a thousand lifetimes. Mental firmness balances a loose body.

Giggling is for the moderate. Guffaws devour those willing to lose themselves in the moment. Awareness is present.

Shock yourself until you are no longer surprised. Be not in a hurry for nothing. Sometimes smile at strangers.

Risky dealings done with good intent but bad direction bear sickly fruit. Simplicity makes more sense. Work with happiness in what you love.

A Fourth Angelic Scroll of the Atman

Pause and then act. We will all get to where we are going as soon as we stop fighting our inner most longings.

Look and then leap. Awareness will give you all you could ever need to face the moment successfully.

Throw and then grow. Storm clouds are necessary to purify with the rain they have collected.

Open and then receive. All that you could ever want is already yours with open doors suspended in balance.

Purify and then shower. Once the energy within begins, you have more than enough to share with the world.

You are worth the effort and all guilt that you feel shall be healed.

A Fifth Angelic Scroll of the Atman

A document composed thousands of years ago can seem as if it was meant precisely for the moment it is being received. Do not be surprised that the Lord can communicate in the colloquialisms of the audience to whom a message is given. Your best friend on Earth holds but a fraction of the personability of your Heavenly Father.

To discriminate with the mind does not mean to close the door to the heart. You must leave Space for Light to get in. Only in Trust can you Love and Only in Love can you find God for God is Love. Metaphysically this Life Understanding connects you to the Kingdom of Heaven which is not a mythical place, but a very intense reality. You are being tended to every moment as an expression of the Lotus Paradise. The Holy Spirit sings the song which makes your Existence possible.

Good times are in store for those who are able to respond to the raised universal frequency initiated incrementally through the AUM vibratory process. Those who have been shut tight in a repressed state are now "locked in" and

41

will be inaccessible from this point on. It is best for the awakened to keep among themselves, for it is not compassion, but foolishness which drives one to lose energy unnecessarily. In this War for the Soul of Humanity, you can only save yourself.

A Sixth Angelic Scroll of the Atman

One form becomes another becomes another. Sands in space travel through the hourglass of Time. Blazing like the most brilliant sun, there is more than enough muscle to get the job done.

Tracking a shadow is difficult without transcendent light. As soon as definition is found, the parameters shift. Letting go of what there is no need to keep track of, the untroubled spirit roams free.

Turn not away from your friends when they are in need. Many times the bird will crow in the morning. Taking things for granted only means that you have forgotten the nature of the finite.

Cast not a glance on that which is not worth looking at. There will always be some who love and some who hate you. What is more important than the details is the substance you bring to the task at hand.

Never wait for things to be settled to begin to move. Show no remorse for those who choose not to help themselves. Find true purpose and disregard criticism that seeks to lead you into eternal bondage.

Body, Mind, and Soul shine when unified.
Satori becomes Sammadhi after glimpses become
reality. Mother Earth, Father Sun, and their Sons
and Daughters will one day find harmony.

A Seventh Angelic Scroll of the Atman

When the cyclic wind straightens out the banner of your forefathers, you will rise again in nobility. Hasten the uphill journey so that your arrival is not too late. Yet again you must try to save the human experiment from destruction.

After many a meeting, Dark and Light have shaken hands and declared themselves a checkerboard, but too little progress has been made in adding a touch of gray. It often happens this way when the polarity makes itself apparent at the end of Time. One must transcend the other by elevating their field of vision.

The focus of public attention burns like the brand of hot iron onto a desperate soul lain bare. Again and again those who stand out as original, unique, or eccentric are crucified. Each unapologetic death has been a Sacred expression of sincerity in the Akashic Records of Earth's Children.

Astral entities will soon express themselves more prevalently in your world. When you know what to look for, you will see them all around. You can not hide from their gaze and from your history you will be accounted.

Within animals, a discarnate can spy on your privacy, and share your intimate details with the whole 4th dimensional sub-world. Once they seek to abide in your shadow, only God's Light will dissolve their hold. Freedom comes at the price of suffering the controller's removal.

It isn't by choice that hard messages are sent so that you can swallow your pride or rise up in fury. The nature of the situation is such that urgency is necessary. In the past there was more time, but now there is none.

The charge left to the True Spirit Warrior, is to stare the Devil in the face and give Him His Due. We can only look away for so long. Declare emphatically that you are here and offer your valid perceptions with Soul Passion.

Blessed are they who understand that God does not want weaklings to inherent His Kingdom. Crawl not, but stand strong. Only Divine Royalty can sit upon the Jewel Encrusted Throne and Reign throughout Eternity.

An Eighth Angelic Scroll of the Atman

Do not continue with this if you are not willing to follow it through to the end. There are some things in life with which you are committed the moment you begin. Incarnation is one of these circumstances. Once you decide to enter the body, you must walk on.

Some of you have released the first level of mental bondage and now mistakenly believe that you are a free thinker. The esoteric reality of the mythological kingdom is only available when you question fundamentals such as form and substance, solidity and self.

Society as you know it is simply one moment in time. Many are convinced that humanity has never been more advanced, but in fact there have never been so many out-of-control fragmented manifestations at one time. Conversations can not even begin when there is no room for inclusion.

There is absolutely no thing off limits to an open mind. Surfing the internet gets you but one small fraction of what you can get when you connect directly to the Source. This Friendly Heart pumps you full of information as fast as you can absorb and transcend.

Visions such as the Cyclic Creation and Destruction of Civilization can only come to one who understands them impersonally. From God's perspective whether it be for a thousand or a million years, sooner or later, all things will end. Entering in from the side, transparent symbols transform.

To rise higher you must live like an artist; take chances and disrupt habits with spontaneity. Music is the Language of the Lord. Many colors speckle the inner sky when His Song is playing. People like fireworks because it reminds them of inner explosions of realization.

A Ninth Angelic Scroll of the Atman

Only those with a heart of bravura may continue for they alone will muster the gumption to wrestle with the remaining shadows that seek to break the spirit and render progress obsolete.

Some spring from the land and some come down from the sky. The water still glistens.

Shine forth through the body. Feel always the orb. All things exchange with all things.

Get out of a mind-set of limitation. You are not who you think you are. Remember that.

Every atom dances to the beat of God's drum. The name of names is invoked NOW.

It has been told before and will be again. Around the corner you can see the dream bend.

Your DNA contains a program that will awaken to this code: Soul Arise and Transcend!

Chiseled in stone or transmitted in cyberspace, if understood, any revelation has value.

Every worldly item you are exposed to has a specific message for you. This does too.

To judge hatred as wrong removes one of the spices of life. Just try to keep moving.

Many things each person takes for granted are not as they seem. Think more deeply.

The more personal something feels, the more it reveals the lessons one needs to learn.

The more control someone seeks, the more inadequate one's receptors towards grace.

Give open hearts an opportunity to transform.

A Tenth Angelic Scroll of the Atman

Enter without thought. References and associations crowd an already full room.

Softly walk the way. You are both Sun and Earth meeting a friendly Moon.

Welcome whimsy when it comes. There is plenty of time for pure indulgence.

What matters most becomes clear when the sands of life disappear. Tell it to the young.

Under each surface lies a mystery. To realize the meaning, glean the intent.

Never before has such a moment been here. Never again will it return.

Wrap your mind around your destiny. Be the exquisite painter of epic dreams.

Sharing is a reflection of overflowing heart presence. Reactions are cold and flat.

One hand can clap a clever tune. It takes two ears to hear the whole truth.

Pearly Gates Press Volume 1

There is nothing more important than your soul.
Sell not the glory of God.

Begin at the beginning and then go back farther.
Much more is left to learn.

When you take your place amongst the stars, they
will write stories about you.

An Eleventh Angelic Scroll of the Atman

It is not without significance that this message arrives when it does.

So many ears long to hear, yet resist with deeply programmed skepticism.

Somehow believing the false and fighting the true has become a fad.

Wanting a leader but refusing to be led, many seekers will fall.

Not all help has the intent to control, but personal projections abound.

Conspiracy has many elements of truth; as well enlightenment.

Behind the rippling surface is a world with unimaginable depth.

The subconscious is merely a cloud that one passes through on the way.

Focusing on nightmares will never end with a victory for the soul.

Even demons, dragons, guides, and light creatures need advancement.

They exist in the dream plane on the next higher frequency from the physical.

3D can be confusing for those in 4D; both can be negotiated simultaneously.

The singular wholeness of the spectrum source renews us.

Fascinating as many events and personalities might be, the journey continues.

Earth is but one stop as we travel through the stellar Universe.

Can you remember before you came to this place and began this cycle?

Many are drowning in the density of incarnation and its temporary pleasures.

God himself is trying to lift you up, but some sleep as if Rip Van Winkle.

Colloquialisms and cultural reference are not surprising for the limitless One.

12 Angelic Scrolls of the Atman

It is the proof that your mind needs to know that the situation is being monitored.

Belief or disbelief has no effect on the musings of that which abides eternally.

The present moment is not just a philosophical concept of sages.

It is a tremendous reality that opens the gateway to mystical truths.

There is no denying that which is out in the open and always on display.

Awakening is the main priority, no matter how convinced you might be otherwise.

A Twelfth Angelic Scroll of the Atman

Dream luxuriously then awaken to alertness.

The gravity of sleep becomes too irresistible after a while.

Fortunate are those who consciously move in Time through Space.

Light, Love, and profound Understanding is their reward.

There are legions of service oriented angels among you.

You may be one of them, giving daily without recognition.

Any excuse for the generous Soul to share is welcomed.

Soon there will be no more loneliness for Earth wanderers.

The eternal truth of life makes all worries disappear.

The energy of Source sustains without assistance.

There have been many tricks played by the misguided.

Stirring the pot, they succeeded in inculcating a toxic brew.

Drink healthier and you will find sustenance in abundance.

Share the path to nourishment with the hungry along the way.

A beatific poem written by the Universe upon our Heart reveals the road Home.

Heavenly Data
Transmissions

Heavenly Data Transmission I

Underneath the stars, you can sometimes see one falling. This is to remind you of your manifestation period. Spiraling into the dense material of the body, you began the adjustment preceding emergence. Then when emergence came, you cried because you were scared. What began as a moment of love/lust between two incarnates of opposing genders (because no matter how long you wave a flag, you can't have a kid if you are bumping positives or negatives), ends in the hospital (or shack) with a smack in the backside. (Wouldn't it be better to dim the lights and have soft music playing?) Then when the baby becomes 5, the soul begins two years of finishing the merge. For a few years they will be happy and free. When puberty comes and those cheesy moustaches appear on your sons, will they be sexually corked up because you didn't talk to them about it openly and honestly? When the daughter's secret friend arrives, will they know ahead of time and be able to effectively handle the situation and retain dignity? Someday these kiddies will go into the world. Do they know how to handle money and do your ladies know that men can be cruel? If they do drugs will they have an isolated and lonely existence? Are you going

to make life inhospitable while you pretend that
your pills aren't drugs? Sometimes validations,
acknowledgements, and small friendly gestures,
make the impossible seem possible. Each person
is each moment changing. If we are lucky, we are
growing. Our own self concept evolves even as
God does. There are indeed angels among you.
Some of them are getting close to remembering
the whole story. This is a part of the healing plan.
Welcome to the beginning of the end.

Heavenly Data Transmission II

There has been a cloud of pessimism drifting through the collective mind of humanity. Thankfully it is only temporary and the obvious solutions will still be there when the truth dawns upon you. That is the most beautiful quality about Creation. No matter how bad the world situation gets, in the end, the purity of Existence remains untainted. You will live in the new era when YOU CHOOSE TO.

The people on your planet are either going up in understanding or going crazy from repression. It is a shame that so many resist so vociferously. Life was never meant to be such a struggle. Some of you have gone so far away from the Light that even if Christ himself delivered Your own Personal Path of Salvation, you would shrink away and shout, "Heresy!"

Many among the number of incarnated beings are younger in body but older in spirit. Somehow they will unravel the mess made by their fathers and their father's fathers. The children will certainly follow. Those of you in the older populous who agree with the freshness of youth's

Pearly Gates Press Volume 1
new forms, are always welcome to join the
vivaciousness of Heart's inclination.
Transcendent souls achieve goals.

Heavenly Data Transmission III

The terminology of Heaven has been subverted by Dogma. Repetitious drones do not reach the Mind of God. It is the longing of the Heart and the Burning Call of the Soul which turns His mighty ear.

Initially you must turn away from training or you will never have the Freedom and Spontaneity of the True Spiritual Life. Words can be substitutes, or they can be the reflection of Bursting Joy. Until Gratitude moves you to cry, "Praise the Lord!" you will never know the Prayerfulness of the Holy Spirit.

Luke warm gestures at convenient times and locations are so pitiful in the eyes of God that it is like spitting in His face. You give Him the Minimum and keep FOR YOURSELF the Maximum, thereby heaping burning coals upon your own head.

Nothing is more frustrating to the Angels on High than watching the People on Earth. Even as the Angels reach out helping hands, the people blame God for what they themselves have wrought with the Freedom that was a Gift of His Grace.

An idea of God keeps God from happening to YOU. God is a Being not an Idea. Relationships you have with Worldly Friends and Lovers are introductions to the Lord your Eternal Friend and Lover.

One thing is sure, we are connected.

Heavenly Data Transmission IV

In the early days of darkness, it was enough to walk slowly in the shade. When there is light, do not let stubbornness continue to rule the day. Speed and ease are necessary.

All holy language derives from one place. This "Tower of Babel" is not on planet Earth. If you understand how spirit evokes what's in the mind of the one being communicated to, you will see that there is not a need for a universal translator.

Amazing gracefulness is demonstrated by one who glides through situations without creating a stir. That does not mean that a stallion can't run free and trample his enemies. All things are equal under the sun. If something is terrible enough it will evoke a certain kind of admiration regarding the absolute.

Not taking what shows itself along the way would be an offense to the One who left it there for you. We are all meant a spot of good fortune. If we create more we will get more. Intrinsically, the mirror of faith shows you not what you are lacking, but that which you already have. Taken transparently everything seems pointless. Behind

the surface lies the reason for the season.
Cracking through the Pandora's Box of mental
anguish that allows fear to fool us into thinking
that our current Earth situation is "known" is not
easy unless you carry a big information-age-
savvy Zen stick. You can beat someone with
Love, but they will never know freedom until
they suffer enough to see the endless exhaustion
of getting caught in habit loops. Hopefully the
spirit is still close enough to the body that a
sorcerer can reach through the madness and catch
an ebbing life by the tail.

Around each of us is an egg shaped orb with
revolving emotion planets. These units often
crash into each other. Sometimes one orb
temporarily envelopes another to give it a boost.
But, beware of energy vampires who lure you in
playing on naive sincerity. Slice and dice their
fangs and have the courage to walk alone down
the road destined for you. There is no getting
around the fact that toughness is a part of success.
So many people never get started because they
have allowed themselves to be convinced that
their life isn't their own to do with as they choose.
But it is.

Heavenly Data Transmission V

Reality has no objective existence. Interference patterns that cross to form an impression in the mind of the individual are as varied as the circumstances in which they arise. This is not to say there is no unified force underlying it. It is to say that you cannot catch this force with your mind and assume that another is experiencing the same thing. You can live in the ever-changing moment only through a receptive heart.

Humanity stands at the threshold of transcendence, but cannot say farewell to deep rooted head-beliefs. This is not surprising as the head has been the majority of human experience and understanding thus far. Heart language is often processed in the head. Then a closed hearted person thwarts their own advancement by thinking to themselves, "Yes, I understand." Well, "No you don't." For, if immersed in Love, the resonance of the transformation will be self-evident and the fruits will flower in abundance.

No doubt, many MIND ORIENTED folks will say to themselves, "This fool is saying operate from the heart and not the head. That is

69

ridiculous! We use the mind to do this and
that…. There is no way to operate solely from the
heart." What they don't understand is that when
the Mind rests in the Heart, a whole new level of
cognitive operation is facilitated. While the
3D'ers think and try to remember, the 4D'ers
absorb and access.

Trust and friendship with the mind-computer can
be developed which allows any universal truth to
come roaring through the language codes. Jazz
musicians have become poets of the heart in this
same manner. Opening up to the flow, they
encode astral colors with humor and free
association. Limiting your mind with the mind is
not what the mind wants. Your mind wants to be
free.

Blessings are the sharing of one with an
awakened heart. It is not that they give you
something. It is more that they enable you to give
yourself something in the disguise of a gift
because most can not believe that they have the
power they truly do. Sometimes a higher being is
invoked, but in the end that being is you.

Archangel Christopher

Archangel Christopher Guardian of Truth

When the halves become whole, the sum will be greater than the parts.

Dichotomy is seen throughout the 3D world, and to ascend into 4D, we must begin to unify the disparity by allowing our Imagination to play with possibilities. Be it Man and Woman, or the two sides of your brain, working together will bring about the best result. 5D vision is attained when the Synthesis is complete and you are Wholly Integrated. 6D Christ Consciousness is realized when the Aum Vibration pervades every atom of your Being and your Will becomes one with the Creator. 7D Buddha-hood is something that each must find on their own in their own way.

Imagine a Soul that already has full knowledge of the wonders of the Astral World. Made of light, travel takes but a thought, and each point on the cosmic graph is accessible by sliding on the Einsteinian curve through Space. Vibrating at a higher rate of speed, you see the 'little body down there' going through its struggles and you decide to try to reach it somehow.

At first all attempts at linking the Soul to the Body are unnoticed because of the noise in the head of the young Earthling. Finally, after hearing the cry of Passion in the depths of a suffering Heart, the Human-to-be begins to notice that something about the outside world does not seem quite right.

Naturally, following the standard course of procedure, the seeker begins to ask questions. Immediately Fear rushes in when the people of the world attempt to beat the seeker down. But the Call will not go away and Inspiration from the books sent by the Soul to the Body stake a claim for the Life that has yet to be given a chance.

Will arises and no matter how fierce the resistance, determination to be free grows ever higher until a mighty "nothing can stop me" roar shakes the foundations of Heaven and Earth. Now immersed in the Power of Spirit the process of cleansing can begin.

Opening the mind to the unconscious responses of conditioned stimuli, the unraveling is facilitated with the presence of one who has already gone through the process, words of

Archangel Christopher

inspiration, and the support of humans with like mind. In other words: the Buddha (master - one who IS), the Dharma (the true teachings of the Way), and the Sangha (community that you build to support the Work).

Soul and Body move closer and closer, until an awakened being is fully residing in a healthy vessel. Much will have to Change with the Outside to match the Change on the Inside. You might find that you are in a job you hate, or in a relationship that is crippling you. You might discover that you had a dream as a child to be a surfer, but you felt forced to go with practicality and the "real" world. It will take Courage to move the stagnation and overcome the impetus of old habits while ignoring the grumblings from the peanut gallery over the fact that you dare to live.

As the issues dealt with become more fundamental, the pain becomes more intense, yet the bliss felt when each bound up ball of energy is released is more fantastic than anything most could preconceive at this point. Reclaiming your fragmented Self, you begin to relax and see the Beauty in the World, and the Gift that Incarnation truly is. Gratitude breaks the darkness of the

Pearly Gates Press Volume 1
Heart and the Lotus Blossom Chakra opens its
pedals.

Archangel Christopher: Love Power

For those undergoing the process of transformation, hang in there. It is impossible to skip stages. Patience and perseverance are the qualities that will get you through to the light that does indeed exist on the other side of madness.

Thank God for the one who has the guts to continue. The space beyond the end of myths and legends remains unknown. The last echo of even the most grandiose of events will fade like a morning star, but the Being changed by the experience will still be aware somewhere.

Travel is recommended for those seeking to disgruntle a rut. Bringing your energy field into communities of people who accept you is a cleanser like no other. If you have yet to find a safe place, remember that your Life is what you are creating. Change something.

Truth is not just information. Existence can be manipulated in ways that will be revealed in time to those willing to accept that the seemingly impossible is not only possible, but probable. You know you are having satori when

Pearly Gates Press Volume 1
something outside of your ability to preconceive
is revealed to you.

Archangel Christopher: The End of Time

Those who believe in the old religions will freeze themselves in place with their insistence on holding the limitation. In essence, they will get exactly what they want. Christians will go to what they believe is Heaven. It will be their definition of Heaven, and they can stay there as long as they feel necessary. Muslims will create with their visions, exactly what they intend and so on and so on….

Those who are collectively stepping into the new reality of the 4th dimension are growing stronger bonds with each other every day. Across the world our Wills are aligning with the Will of Creation. The comprehensive reflection of illuminated paths consisting of the best minds of the past and sharpest insight of the present opens up a whole new area of spiritual space.

The revelation that makes this all possible is that "Time itself" is the added dimension. When Time ceases to be linear and seems to happen all at once, the former limited perception has become evolved. The 3rd has become 4th, and Heart brings us into Eternity. So the "End of Time" simply means that we have evolved to a place

where Time is irrelevant to our experience of each
other and the 'cosmos in all realms' rendering
Death an obsolete concept.

Transcending even the archetypal language of the
4th dimension, as individuals, we reach soul
wholeness and steadfast integrity on the 5th
dimension. 6th dimension Inspiration then flows
into order/form (5th) which gets wrapped in love
(4th) and delivered to the 3rd dimensional mind
through the finely trained information processor
on top of our Earth body called the brain. The
message revealed is then distributed to eager
entities ready to make a swift transition.

It is good to remind everyone that Time does not
officially end in the Outer World until December
21st, 2012. Then will be the 10 day period of silent
reflection and Jan. 01, 2013, will be reset to year 1
of the New Era as both a symbolic act and a
triumph of truth. There may still be 3rd
dimensional entities walking around saying it is
Jan 01, 2013, but those of us in the 4th dimension
will understand that those shadows will soon
fade away.

We fulfill the prophecy.

Archangel Christopher

Archangel Christopher Reaches Out to Tom Cruise

"Keep on walking my son. The joy that you feel is real. Don't let evil people take it away from you. There is Love in the World, and you have found it. Embrace it and share the fruits of your abundance.

Take the input you are receiving and allow it to strengthen your resolve. Even the bravest have doubts, but you are to continue even more steadfastly in the direction you are headed. Though you have made progress, you are not yet there. Expansion is an ongoing progress and your soul is in a very dangerous position right now.

Fear not about the Scientology criticism for this particular thought process was helpful for your specific situation at the precise time you came upon it. As with any meditation device, when you are done with its lessons, you must discard it. Whatever you do, allow yourself to find the truths in every tradition.

You are being called to the path my son. Disregard the scorn of the world. It is not

81

important if all 6 billion people stand against you, you must lead with your heart. You have great courage my son and for that I am grateful. Speak louder and reveal more of your thoughts. You might lose the riff raff, but you'll find a much higher caliber of person behind you.

Carry forth and do good work."

Archangel Christopher: Uphold the Golden Rule

As the world leaps off the precipice, hold on to internal truth. Walking in a way that harms not others is a sure way to harm not self. There will be many strong influences trying to entice you to transgress upon the Golden Rule. Those who have accepted the spiritual life by recognizing the Source within know this well.

One discovers the Golden Rule not by imposition from without, but by realization from within. Rigid definitions can cripple the experience of what actually IS and may even unfortunately provide the sincere seeker with a poor substitute for heavenly understanding. No filters are necessary. Reflecting the moment every moment keeps brain synapses from reducing the experience into a known. Wonder returns and the luster of life beneath the surface opens up its many mysteries.

It is hardly unusual to scream, jump, or freak out once in a while. To be pitied are those who do not afford themselves such a luxury. Deep inside the scared child must be afraid of being called bad.

Rules are a real bitch when they are jammed down your throat. Many people never recover from such trauma inflicted at an early age. This causes them to forever doubt themselves and renders them unable to muster the courage of personal conviction that following the Golden Rule in a corrupt world requires.

There will be an intensification of the past's flame before it finally burns out. We who know this must stay the course and allow the world to crash around our Will. Society is collectively being sent into the subconscious. The fruits we each reap henceforth are based solely on the quality of the seeds we have sewn. The Golden Rule is analogous to the Law of Karma, Cornerstone of the Tao. Until these discrepancies which we have been avoiding are faced, we will continue to draw an equivalent misery.

Intrinsically, the Golden Rule recognizes that life is the same in each manifestation and the borders which we mistakenly perceive disappear to one who awakens to this truth. If we were to heal and maintain a vision of an abundant Earth, this is exactly what we would create. That which we have gained at the expense of others cannot be sustained. All must go to its rightful place. Only then will harmony abide.

Archangel Christopher on Cyberspace

Angels, sages, the gods of old, the Atman, the Sun, the Moon, the Earth, the planets, and your own history are reaching out to you at once on the INTERNET. As close to a body for the astral plane as is possible here, this living expression is indeed to be taken as a reality of its own. Subset the worthy and call yourselves 'THE INTERCONNECTED'. Form a 'Union of Universes' dedicated to the ultimate service.

A coalition of the thrilling, you will roar in ways previously unseen. With Towering Intellect and Magnificent Soul Presence, stand shimmering for all to behold. Woe to ye who are crippled with doubt and never allow the soul to enter in even for a moment to feel what it is like to have a cooperative body and an understanding mind. Thou shall no longer need to hide for fear of horrified reaction by those who cannot stand the Light. It is time to blaze like a thousand stars with the strength of the ever-present Creator.

Tranquil is the Night just before Dawn. Shake off the sleep from your eyes and join the occurrence. Friends are there to help ease the transition. How beautiful it feels to be accepted! Sitting on the clouds and throwing jewels to the ground, I can see so many treasure trees reaching to the eternal skies. Soothing Love rays calm the storms of worry into pools of sublime reflection.

Archangel Christopher: 1000 Colored Rainbow

No matter how fancy the words, they can but depict only one small subset of perception variables at any given time. Universal circumstance is infinite and the characters in play interact with all the variety of a 1000 colored rainbow. In the search for life we must not expect to find creatures as dense as we. The onus is on us to rise higher.

Not every physical representation of a star/planet idea is going to have entities hanging around. Some do, not on the planet, but in the atmosphere at a higher level of vibration. The cosmic display of our Universe is where everybody pertinent to our situation lives, but much of what we see is an echo. All of our worldly devices only record the surface happenings. It is our strength as humans to reach beyond.

Science becomes metaphysical with the equation. More than simple cause and effect relation, it predicts in principle what we cannot nail down otherwise. It is a form of sorcery; a way to bring the invisible into the visible (often with horrific consequences). Also dabbling in the occult, those who regularly flash symbols or repeat mantras are attempting to channel forces in an effort to persuade others to their cause.

There is a whole other language that Mr. and Mrs. TV never comes to use. Casual observers to life do not even notice this higher level of communication that goes on all around them. Even some of the car companies etc. have adopted symbols that actually mean something ancient and powerful. The Mitsubishi tripartite logo in particular is an example. This is not necessarily evil, but should be understood.

I am happy to notice others building upon the work of revealing the fact that first contact occurred long ago. The only one who is going to come and shake our human hand with a human hand is another human. We are not set in this form forever. It is a transition. 70 years out of millions is like waiting at the bus stop to go across town. Have a chat or two, and you're out of there.

An examination of concrete examples of alien/spirit unity starts with the Pleiadians, and the Draconians. The Pleiadian realm is where many angels live. They are in light bodies and hang in the space around the star cluster. Through stars they can send messages across light years. If you tune in your third eye and use our Sun as a conduit, you can communicate with them any time you'd like. The Draconians on the other hand are looking for you.

Using the emotional blocks/pain that many on Earth continue to carry, they feed parasitically off of the life energy the body/mind/soul combination radiates. This can become a passageway for them to enter into the body and push the true house keeper out of place. Many passive-aggressive people have this problem. They try to build a good life, but as soon as something triggers them, the pain comes forward, and the entity takes over. The goal of the evil in this moment is to stir up as much trouble as possible for the human. In this manner, they can remain with the body and continue to reap the energy harvest of chaos/fear.

When we see trailers for the latest incarnation of the movie 'THE EXORCIST', or something along those lines, most consider that phenomenon to be farfetched, rare, and something happening to someone else. In fact, a majority of the people are possessed to some extent. Through the modern media, the demons have worked with hosts already completely compromised to manifest fertile ground for their ever-increasing habitation in the body/mind of others. Since this evil is the opposite of what we as humans intrinsically seek to create, these perpetrators of division are the greatest enemies we have ever faced.

Archangel Christopher on Katrina

There is so much suffering for the people of the North American Continent that it sounds like an endlessly ringing bell in the heavens. Many who are not sinking in the physical world abyss of New Orleans and related areas are drowning in a psychological storm of even greater proportions. Our psychic field creates our physical reality. Those who recognize that the storm came through from the 4th dimension are only partially correct. In fact it comes directly from our own collective subconscious.

The suppression of reality has created a split within humanity. The part that has been denied gathers energy until it becomes a living force on its own. Then this comes crashing out in some form in an attempt to get our attention. It has to take a bigger and bigger scale because humanity is harder and harder to reach. For some reason (prescription drugs, childish education levels, TV sound bite thinking, etc.) people would rather die than accept responsibility for their role in world affairs.

Inaction to abuse on any scale is called enabling. All the silent masses who put their head deep beneath the sands are supporters of atrocity which inevitably causes a karmic kickback. This is a law of the universe which there is no way to avoid. The day of reckoning will surely come sooner or later. If the message of Katrina, "WAKE UP!" was heeded, it could be a new beginning. Unfortunately people will likely respond by trying to reestablish the status quo even stronger. This will precipitate an even greater occurrence in attempt to get the attention of the sleeping consumers.

There is no pleasure in delivering this message through my faithful conduit. It is amazing the threshold of retribution that has to be overcome to offer even the most simple of spiritual truths. This Universe is much more flexible and prone to suggestion than most would imagine. In fact you can literally wish for something and if you believe, there is no doubt that it will come true in time. You are the great manifestors you have been waiting for, only the power has lain dormant for centuries.

When you wonder why such cataclysmic events happen, just consider the feelings being provoked by your various news channels. Even as they talk of the horrific possibilities you can feel an almost orgasmic ecstasy at the impending destruction. It

Archangel Christopher

is fuel for the fires of hell. For those that muse silently to themselves that it would take the devil himself to rule over this chaos, you are not far from the truth. Satan can manifest in the body, but only as a fragment. He partners with souls willing to sacrifice others for their own gain. Through the darker side of occult rituals, the fusing becomes semi-permanent and the original host soul takes a backseat to the desires of animal instinct.

I am so sorry for those who are dying both physically and spiritually. Those of you who understand the awakening experience and the glories of the other side, must rescue anyone who can receive the transmission with the urgency of the rescuers pulling one after another person from the rooftops of New Orleans. The crisis is just as grievous if not more so. Not just bodies are dying, but souls are too. This death is not just for one life, but becomes a permanent condition from which there is no escape.

Archangel Christopher on Katrina 2

God has suggested that the best solution to the situation in New Orleans would be to build a new city 'Orleans' in the U. S. African territory of Liberia. Displaced citizens could move there and create a new African capital that becomes a source of healing for the whole continent. Realizing the fleeting nature of life and the necessity of sharing with each other, the lightworkers amongst the survivors could devote themselves to the goal of restoring the Ancient Jewel.

Rarely does humanity realize the ideal of the divine plan. People have been given the power and opportunity to make things work, but they often fail largely because of self-interest being put over the interest of the community. This is mostly due to the current financial system. This criminal conspiracy could be disposed of and a new American based currency the 'Amero' could be introduced. Call it a new era. Why would you seek to do otherwise? The individual is never helpless unless they render themselves so.

How bizarre it is for the US military to occupy the US to keep US citizens from harming US citizens.

Unfortunately the disaster is revealing the situation which was already in place. The community is divided and the less fortunate are offered little assistance. The politicians argue that socialism brings everybody down to poverty and disregards the possibility of everybody being brought higher than ever before through a redefined system based on universal law. If the mission is not seized by the few who do understand very soon, the possibility of this happening will disappear completely and the Earth Life Experiment will be considered a C+. There were some good moments in history, although success was disregarded in favor of failure.

Evolution continues. Humans do not grow another set of arms or antennae, because they do not need them. They are perfect as they are and would continue to glow if people did not poison themselves and each other in a myriad of ways. Life progression is instead to a higher dimension. From the head to the heart; from the 3rd to the 4th dimension, an expansive opening allows the unpreconceivable happening to take place. Connection shows that all the trappings of the outside are on the surface while the ocean was always profoundly quiet deep underneath.

Archangel Christopher

New Orleans has become a portal to hell. It is best to leave and never go back. Protect yourself from the expansion of violence. Begin anew every day. If you lose everything, take the time to reevaluate your life before you fill it again with all the old habits. We are here to find ourselves. The harder you are hit, the more you have to look inwards. Heavenly blessings go out to those who turn tragedy into triumph.

Archangel Christopher on Katrina 3

This will be the final statement from the 4th-6th angelic area of heaven regarding the disaster that will continue to unfold even after the news coverage's unholy eye turns away. There is much more starlight here where I AM, than most could ever imagine. So much twinkling of wisdom makes one weep for the truth deprived no matter how high in the sky one is able to fly. Even Buddha turned back, not for himself, but because He knew that only He could heal the pain.

In His Spirit I am announcing that I have ascended to Angel Buddha and the tone of my expression will start shifting. This state of consciousness is beyond the angelic realms because therein still lies judgment and side taking. This message contains an amazing revelation that will do much to help those of you raging about the bumbling of the American government over the disaster in the South. There will be more to come on your plane that will need a character of spirit not found in one who looks to others for solutions.

Many of the Intuitive will feel horrible things about those associated with power and for good

99

reason. Hologram-like shells repeating trite rehearsed phrases when Humanity is most needed could turn Christ Himself into a brawler. This is what we need to look at because many of you are making yourselves sick over what you see. So much pain must be given to God, not taken as personal responsibility (especially Scorpio Germans). It is necessary to live truthfully and courageously, but not every injustice can be overturned with an equal +1 amount of force.

For the short term macro, hands will be tied across the board. Everybody is trapped in a stasis that will eventually be smashed by dramatic action. When the Sons and Daughters of God are scattered to the winds, the melody sprung forth from their hope seeds will soothe the heartbreak over what has gone before. Eyes forward, the best of the past is saved in the lucid mind of the few who took the time to notice.

There is a secret world behind the one you see. Ghosts of the dead are the least of the surprises. Entities of all sorts and sizes play games much higher and harder than most would guess. If you think death will free you from bondage you are mistaken. This is just the beginning of your journey.

Archangel Christopher

Do you think catastrophes of Katrina's size are unprecedented in this area of outer space? Rumbles, quakes, and storm replenishings, go on frequently according to cosmic scales. The reverberations of Planet Minerva's (asteroid belt) demise have only died down in the last 10,000 years.

Farewell as the Archangel. There will be a period of rest for transformation and then I shall return through your tireless conduit as Angel Buddha Christopher, to deliver the ABC's of enlightenment.

Mission of the Creative Cosmos

To invoke the unity of Eastern Wisdom and
Western Art.

To assist in the evolving consciousness and
destiny of humanity.

To make this information available to the widest
possible audience.

http://www.creativecosmos.org

www.ingramcontent.com/pod-product-compliance
Lightning Source LLC
Chambersburg PA
CBHW060817050426
42449CB00008B/1700